MACHINES THAT WON THE WAR

MACHINES AND WEAPONRY OF THE GULF WAR

Charlie Samuels

Gareth Stevens
Publishing

Please visit our website, www.garethstevens.com. For a free color catalog of all our high-quality books, call toll free 1-800-542-2595 or fax 1-877-542-2596.

Library of Congress Cataloging-in-Publication Data

Samuels, Charlie, 1961-
 Machines and weaponry of the Gulf War / Charlie Samuels.
     p. cm. — (Machines that won the war)
 Includes index.
 ISBN 978-1-4339-8596-6 (pbk.)
 ISBN 978-1-4339-8597-3 (6-pack)
 ISBN 978-1-4339-8595-9 (library binding)
 1. Persian Gulf War, 1991—Equipment and supplies. 2. Weapons systems. I. Title.
 DS79.744.S34S36 2012
 956.7044'24—dc23

                          2012024373

Published in 2013 by
Gareth Stevens Publishing
111 East 14th Street, Suite 349
New York, NY 10003

For Brown Bear Books Ltd:
Editorial Director: Lindsey Lowe
Managing Editor: Tim Cooke
Children's Publisher: Anne O'Daly
Art Director: Jeni Child
Designer: Lynne Lennon
Picture Manager: Sophie Mortimer
Production Director: Alastair Gourlay

Picture Credits
Front Cover: U.S. Department of Defense

All photographs: U.S. Department of Defense.

Manufactured in the United States of America
1 2 3 4 5 6 7 8 9 12 11 10

CPSIA compliance information: Batch #CW12GS: For further information contact Gareth Stevens, New York, New York at 1-800-542-2595.

CONTENTS

INTRODUCTION 4

A-10 THUNDERBOLT 6

AH-1 SUPERCOBRA 8

AH-64 APACHE 10

B-52 STRATOFORTRESS 12

CHALLENGER TANK 14

E-3 AWACS 16

E-8 JOINT STARS 18

F-15E STRIKE EAGLE 20

F-16 FIGHTING FALCON 22

F-177 NIGHTHAWK 24

HMMWV HUMVEE 26

M1A1 ABRAMS 28

M2/M3 BRADLEY 30

M16A2 RIFLE 32

M109 PALADIN 34

MIM-104 PATRIOT 36

MLRS STEEL RAIN 38

TOMAHAWK MISSILE 40

UAV DRONES 42

WARRIOR INFANTRY FIGHTING VEHICLE 44

GLOSSARY 46

FURTHER INFORMATION 47

INDEX 48

INTRODUCTION

The buildup to the Gulf War of 1991 had begun in August 1990. The Iraqi dictator, Saddam Hussein, had occupied neighboring Kuwait. Led by the United States, the United Nations (UN) condemned the invasion. It formed a coalition of 34 countries to resist it. Military forces gathered in Saudi Arabia.

A British Challenger II tank crosses the Iraqi Desert. Coaltion tanks were superior to the Iraqis' Soviet-built tanks.

Coalition: A temporary alliance of countries to achieve a particular purpose.

The B-117 Nighthawk uses advanced "stealth" technology to defeat enemy radar defenses; here, it drops a guided bomb.

The troop buildup was intended to prevent Saddam Hussein invading Saudi Arabia. The operation was codenamed Operation Desert Shield.

DESERT STORM

The attack phase of the Gulf War, which began in January 1991, was Operation Desert Storm. Supported by Coalition aircraft and artillery that pounded Iraqi positions, ground troops invaded Kuwait. Coalition commanders had expected fierce resistance from Iraqi troops. Instead, the war was over in just a few weeks. Saddam had no answer to the Coalition's superior military hardware. His forces evacuated Kuwait and retreated back to Iraq, under constant Coalition fire.

Artillery: Big guns such as cannons, howitzers, and mortars.

The A-10 can carry Maverick missiles, cluster bombs, or bombs to be dropped by parachute.

A-10 THUNDERBOLT

The A-10 might be the ugliest warplane ever built. It is nicknamed the "Warthog" for its squat body. But it was a star performer during the Gulf War. The U.S. Air Force designed the aircraft for close air support (CAS). It knocks out enemy tanks and other targets to help forces advancing on the ground.

Close air support: Aerial attacks on enemy weapons or troops engaged in ground fighting.

TANK SHREDDER

The Warthog packs a lot of firepower. Its seven-barreled Gruman cannon is the heaviest rotary cannon ever put in a warplane. It fires different types of bombs and missiles. Its tight turning circle and ability to fly at low altitudes helped earn it another nickname: "tank shredder." Warthogs destroyed convoys of Iraqi tanks as they fled Kuwait in February 1991.

The A-10's cockpit is covered in titanium armor so it can stand up to antiaircraft attack. Of the 20 A-10s damaged during the war, only one was unable to carry on flying.

EYEWITNESS

"There were lots of things burning on the ground. The A-10s were in there killing tanks. The Iraqi Army cannot hide. They are being obliterated."

Major Michael Donnelly
U.S. Air Force, Desert Storm

The Warthog has more than 1,200 pounds (540 kg) of armor to reinforce its hull.

The A-10's seven-barreled cannon is the heaviest rotary cannon ever carried on a plane.

Convoy: An organized group of vehicles or ships all following the same route.

AH-1 SUPERCOBRA

The first major battle of the Gulf War was fought at Khafji on January 29–February 1, 1991. U.S. commanders had to win. They sent in their AH-1 SuperCobras. The chopper's three-barreled machine gun is the fastest-firing gun in the world. The SuperCobra took out some of the first Iraqi armored vehicles of the war.

The SuperCobra has a crew of two: a pilot and a copilot who is also the gunner.

Armored: Something that is covered with a hard case for protection against missiles.

A technician loads a high-explosive rocket into a launch unit on a SuperCobra.

STOP GAP

The SuperCobra was originally developed as a stop gap for the U.S. Army to use in the Vietnam War (1963–1973). It proved so reliable that it was put into production. It has been used ever since, serving in Grenada and Beirut before the Gulf War.

A Marine AH-1 SuperCobra prepares to lift off during a medical evacuation mission in the desert.

FLYING ARSENAL

The 78 SuperCobras that were deployed during the war flew 1,273 sorties into Iraq. They suffered no combat losses. Speeding in at up to 207 miles per hour (333 km/h), the attack helicopters destroyed 97 enemy tanks and 104 armored personnel carriers and vehicles, as well as two antiaircraft artillery sites.

The SuperCobra is a flying arsenal. Its machine gun has 750 rounds of ammunition and a 1.2-mile (2-km) range. It carries air-to-air and air-to-ground missiles, and is the only helicopter armed with the Sidewinder air-to-air missile.

Sortie: A military word for a single mission by a single aircraft.

AH-64 APACHE

The Apache is not known as the "flying tank" for nothing. It can carry up to 16 Hellfire missiles. Its fearsome armament made it the U.S. Army's most deadly tank destroyer. Its job was to locate, engage, and destroy enemy armored vehicles. Apaches fired the first shots of Desert Storm.

Apaches carrying folding-fin rockets and Hellfire missiles fly over the desert.

Folding-fin rockets: Rockets with fins that fold flat for storage.

One U.S. general claimed that the Apache could "fire a Hellfire missile through a window from four miles (6.5 km) away at night."

NO ESCAPE

At the end of the war, Iraqi troops fled from Kuwait on the Basra Road. Fleets of Apaches, backed by A-10s, destroyed hundreds of military vehicles. The line of twisted, smouldering wrecks gave the road its nickname: the "Highway of Death."

Night-vision sensors on the helicopter feed data to the pilot's heads-up display for flying in the dark.

VITAL APACHE

Eight AH-64s destroyed part of the Iraqi radar network at the start of the war so that Coalition fighter planes could get into Iraq without being detected. During the 100-hour ground war, 277 Apaches took part. They destroyed more than 500 Iraqi tanks and many armored personnel carriers.

Only one Apache was hit in the war, and its crew survived. Keeping the choppers in the war was critical. The U.S. Army grounded all its Apaches in the rest of the world in case they needed spare parts.

Heads-up display: A system that projects data on a level with the pilot's eyes.

The B-52 has been in service for over 50 years; recent upgrades will keep it in service until the 2040s.

B-52
STRATOFORTRESS

The Gulf War may have been a modern, high-tech conflict, but one of its star performers was an old workhorse. The B-52 has been around since 1954. The bomber was updated from the late 1980s onward. It was given new weapons and used tactics that would destroy Iraqi morale during the Gulf War.

Morale: The spirit of combatants in a war and their belief in whether they can win.

GIANT AIRPLANE

The bombers are huge: They have eight engines and a massive wingspan of 185 feet (56.64 m). The B-52s are ideal for long-range missions. They can fly for around 8,000 miles (12,875 km) before they need to refuel.

During Operation Desert Storm, a total of 86 B-52s flew 1,600 missions. They dropped almost 26,000 tons of bombs (around 29 percent of the total dropped). Two-thirds of the bombs were dropped on Iraqi ground forces. The rest were used against specific targets, such as electrical power plants and military sites.

There are five crew: a pilot, copilot, radar navigator (bombardier), navigator, and an electronic warfare officer.

EYEWITNESS

"The objective of the B-52's role was psychological. It was to undermine the morale of Iraqi ground forces through periodic bombardment."

Official Postwar Study U.S. Air Force

Wingspan: The distance between the two wingtips of an airplane.

CHALLENGER TANK

The British Challenger I tank played a key role in the war on the ground. Challengers knocked out around 300 Iraqi main battle tanks (MBTs) for no losses. The Challengers were dubbed "desert rats," for a British regiment in World War II famous for desert fighting. The tanks had a picture of a red rat painted on their sides.

A Challenger fires a shell from its main gun. The shells have a range of over 3 miles (5 km).

Main battle tanks: The most heavily armed and armored class of tanks.

Challengers accompany a British motorized column in the Kuwaiti desert.

SUPERIOR WEAPON

The Challenger was far superior to enemy tanks. Its state-of-the-art armor was made from a mixture of steel and ceramics to form an almost impenetrable case. It had a range of 373 miles (600 km).

The Challenger's gun had a rifled barrel. This made the gun very accurate. It could hit targets over 3 miles (5 km) away. The tank fired DU (depleted uranium) rounds, which penetrated Iraqi tanks. More than 1,400 of the 3,700 Iraqi tanks destroyed during the war were hit by DU rounds.

Rifled: A barrel with a spiral groove inside that spins a shell and makes its flight more accurate.

E-3 AWACS

The distinctive disk-shaped radar on top of the E-3 revolves six times per minute.

Intelligence is key in any war. All military commanders want to know what the enemy is doing. The E-3 can tell them. The aircraft, also known as the Sentry, is an airborne warning and control system (AWACS). It's like an eye in the sky. The specially adapted Boeing 707s have a super-advanced radar system. In the Gulf War, they meant the U.S. commanders always knew about the movements of Iraqi aircraft.

Radar: A system that locates objects by bouncing radio waves off them.

RADAR SYSTEM

The E-3 is easy to spot thanks to its large disk-shaped radar antenna. The rotating antenna feeds signals to up to 17 crew. In Desert Storm, E-3s logged more than 5,000 hours of surveillance. For the first time ever, an entire war was recorded.

The AWACS detects low-flying aircraft over 200 miles away (320 km) and high-flying airplanes even farther away. It can track hundreds of targets at the same time, so enemy planes can always be intercepted.

The view shows the inside of the cockpit of an E-3 on a nighttime mission.

An E-3 Sentry comes in to land at the end of another mission.

Antenna: An aerial for sending or receiving radio signals.

E-8 JOINT STARS

The Joint Surveillance Target Attack Radar System (Joint STARS) was the newest technology used in the Gulf War. It was developed in the 1980s. It arrived in Saudi Arabia just hours before the war began, at the request of Commander Norman Schwarzkopf. It was one of the great technological successes of the war.

 The E-8 is a modified Boeing 707 airliner. It can fly for nine hours at altitudes of up to 42,000 feet (13,000 m).

Altitude: How high something is above the ground.

Joint STARS was still in development when the war began, but two E-8s were sent to the Gulf.

NIGHT PROWLER

Joint STARS gave Coalition battlefield commanders a vital edge. It revealed all enemy troop, tank, and helicopter movements up to 120 miles (190 km) away.

Every night one of two E-8 aircraft (modified Boeing 707s) flew for up to 12 hours. The plane's radar gathered information that was passed to ground stations. Not only could targets be identified, tracked, and targeted, the system also generated photographic radar. It was particularly good at finding SCUD missile launchers.

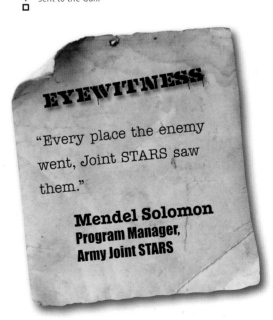

EYEWITNESS

"Every place the enemy went, Joint STARS saw them."

Mendel Solomon
Program Manager,
Army Joint STARS

SCUD: A Soviet-built ballistic missile that the Iraqis launched against Coalition targets.

F-15E STRIKE EAGLE

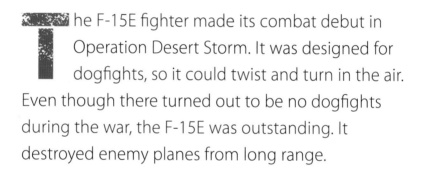

The F-15E fighter made its combat debut in Operation Desert Storm. It was designed for dogfights, so it could twist and turn in the air. Even though there turned out to be no dogfights during the war, the F-15E was outstanding. It destroyed enemy planes from long range.

The F-15E has a crew of two. The pilot is accompanied by a weapons systems operator.

Dogfight: A close-quarters fight between warplanes.

The F-15E was a strike aircraft version of the earlier fighter, the F-15, which was developed in the 1960s.

SUPREME PERFORMANCE

The F-15E strikes quickly. Flying at altitudes of up to 65,000 feet (19,800 m), the planes reach 1,650 miles (2,660 km) per hour, over twice the speed of sound. They are heavily armed with cannons, missiles, and bombs, but the cannon was not fired in Desert Storm. F-15Es shot down 36 enemy aircraft. Mostly they used AIM-7 Sparrow missiles, which work when targets cannot be seen with the naked eye.

A key F-15E mission was to attack Iraqi SCUD missiles. They used special target-detection and night-vision systems to achieve a hit rate of up to 80 percent with their laser-guided bombs.

The F-15E's bombs and missiles hit 2,124 targets during 2,172 sorties over Iraq and Kuwait.

Cannon: A large-caliber, automatic gun on an airplane.

F-16 FIGHTING FALCON

An F-16 is tethered to the ground; when its engines are on full burn, the tether is released and the airplane shoots away to take off.

On January 19, 1991, the largest air strike of the Gulf War took place. Package Q took on the heavy air defenses of the Iraqi capital, Baghdad. At the heart of the strike were 56 F-16s. They caused massive damage on the ground. Two F-16s were shot down and the pilots taken prisoner.

Full burn: The stage where an engine is turned up to its full power.

The mounts beneath the wings of the F-16 can be used to carry a wide range of weapons.

NUMBER ONE AIRPLANE

The multirole F-16s were the most used aircraft in the Gulf War. A total of 249 F-16s flew 13,340 sorties against Iraq.

What made the F-16 special was its immense maneuverability and its combat radius, or the distance it can fly, fight, and return to base. At 340 miles (550 km), this was greater than any other aircraft. The F-16 was also able to find targets in any weather, to fly low, to strike with great accuracy, and to defend itself against enemy aircraft . No wonder it was the number one aircraft of Operation Desert Storm.

Multirole: An aircraft that can act as a fighter or a bomber and attack a variety of targets.

The low shape and angled surfaces of the F-117 lessened the radar signals it reflected.

F-117 NIGHTHAWK

There has never been an airplane like the F-117 Nighthawk. The bomber used the latest stealth technology to be invisible to radar. Its shape and the materials it was made from both deflected radar signals. The bomber could strike deep in enemy territory before the enemy even knew it was there.

Stealth: The name given to technology designed to minimize an object's visibility to radar.

PRECISION BOMBER

The F-117 was still new at the start of the Gulf War. It hadn't been tested in conflict. It was given a specific task: to carry out precision bombing of ground targets in downtown Baghdad, the Iraqi capital.

It was spectacularly successful. Although stealth bombers made up just 2.5 percent of the total number of Coalition aircraft, they hit more than 40 percent of all the strategic targets destroyed. In 1,299 sorties in Operation Desert Storm, not a single F-117 was lost. The F-117 was retired in 2008 as technology made it obsolete.

EYEWITNESS

"I saw a car starting to drive across the bridge, and I aimed behind him. If I had hit the left side of the bridge, he would've driven right into the explosion. Instead I hit the right side. You can pick and choose a little bit in the F-117."

Major Joe Salato
F-117 Pilot

Ground crew prepare a flight of F-117s for another mission.

F-117s fly above the desert in formation.

Strategic: To do with the overall goals of a military campaign, not the immediate fighting.

HMMWV HUMVEE

One of the stars of the ground war in Operation Desert Storm was the High Mobility Multipurpose Wheeled Vehicle—HMMWV, or just Humvee. It replaced the jeep as the U.S. Army's "do everything" vehicle. Twenty thousand Humvees were deployed to the Persian Gulf.

Armored models of the Humvee can withstand armor-piercing missiles and antitank mine blasts.

Mine: An explosive charge buried in the ground that is detonated by weight on top of it.

A Humvee driver takes aim with his squad automatic weapon (SAW).

As the day breaks, heavily packed Humvees prepare to set out on a patrol. The vehicles can carry huge amounts of cargo.

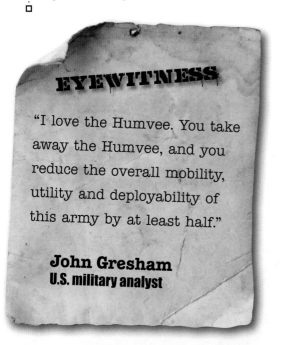

EYEWITNESS

"I love the Humvee. You take away the Humvee, and you reduce the overall mobility, utility and deployability of this army by at least half."

John Gresham
U.S. military analyst

MANY ROLES

The Humvee is a super-tough cross between an SUV and an armored mini-tank. It could go virtually anywhere. Armed with howitzers, mortars, or machine guns, it patrolled the deserts.

What made the Humvee unique was its versatility. It could carry soldiers, be an ambulance or a police car, a reconnaissance vehicle, or be equipped with a radar dish to become a communications platform. After the war, a nonmilitary version became a common sight on U.S. roads.

Deployability: The ability to get military forces into position quickly.

27

M1A1 ABRAMS

When the U.S. Army needs firepower, it sends for the Abrams. The tank's main 120mm cannon can fire a variety of shells, from high explosive to armor piercing. It has a kill range of over 1.5 miles (2,500 m), so it can take out enemies before they are close enough to take a shot themselves.

The Abrams is one of the heaviest tanks in the world. Its thick armor can withstand shells from any other tank.

Kill range: The distance at which a tank can destroy another tank.

Only a handful of Abrams were lost during the conflict; of those only six were confirmed to have been lost to enemy fire.

U.S. soldiers prepare to load 120mm shells into their Abrams tanks.

WHISPERING DEATH

The M1A1 was the main battle tank of the U.S. Army. Troops called it "the Beast," "Dracula," and "Whispering Death." Although it was massively outnumbered—1,800 M1A1s faced 4,200 Iraqi tanks—it performed spectacularly well. Only nine Abrams were lost through war damage.

The Abrams used lasers and onboard computers to calculate range and make its firing as accurate as possible. It fired armor-piercing sabots, metal darts that pierced the enemy tank's armor and then exploded inside.

Laser: A thin, high-powered beam of light used to take measurements.

Both the M2 and the M3 have a crew of three: a commander, a gunner, and a driver.

M2 / M3 BRADLEY

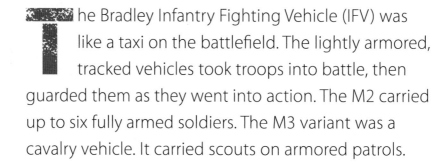

The Bradley Infantry Fighting Vehicle (IFV) was like a taxi on the battlefield. The lightly armored, tracked vehicles took troops into battle, then guarded them as they went into action. The M2 carried up to six fully armed soldiers. The M3 variant was a cavalry vehicle. It carried scouts on armored patrols.

Scouts: Soldiers trained to go into enemy territory to gather information.

INFANTRY SUPPORT

The Bradleys were armed to support the infantry. They carried a launcher for the TOW-2 antitank guided missile and a 25mm M242 Bushmaster cannon. They were not intended to fight tanks, but they destroyed more Iraqi tanks than M1A1 tanks did.

The Bradleys were the workhorses of the ground war. With a top speed of 41 miles per hour (66 km/h), they kept the U.S. advance moving fast. Of the 220 Bradleys deployed, only three broke down, even in sandstorms that blew grit into the engine.

EYEWITNESS

"The Bradley is a well-armed, armored battle taxi designed to deliver a squad of infantry or a team of scouts to the edge of a battlefield, support them with fire as necessary, and then re-embark them for movement under armor to the next objective."

Tom Clancy
Armored Cav (1996)

A Bradley M2 provides cover while infantry carry out a patrol on the streets of a town in the Middle East.

Guided missile: A missile that can be steered toward its target.

M16A2 RIFLE

Anyone who has been in the U.S. Army in the last 50 years knows the M16. The rifle and its variants, including the A2, has been standard issue for U.S. troops since the Vietnam War of the 1960s. All U.S. infantry, and their Saudi and Kuwaiti allies, carried the M16 during Operation Desert Storm.

This version of the M16A2 has a laser-aiming device mounted above the front grip.

Automatic: A gun that fires continuously while the trigger is pulled.

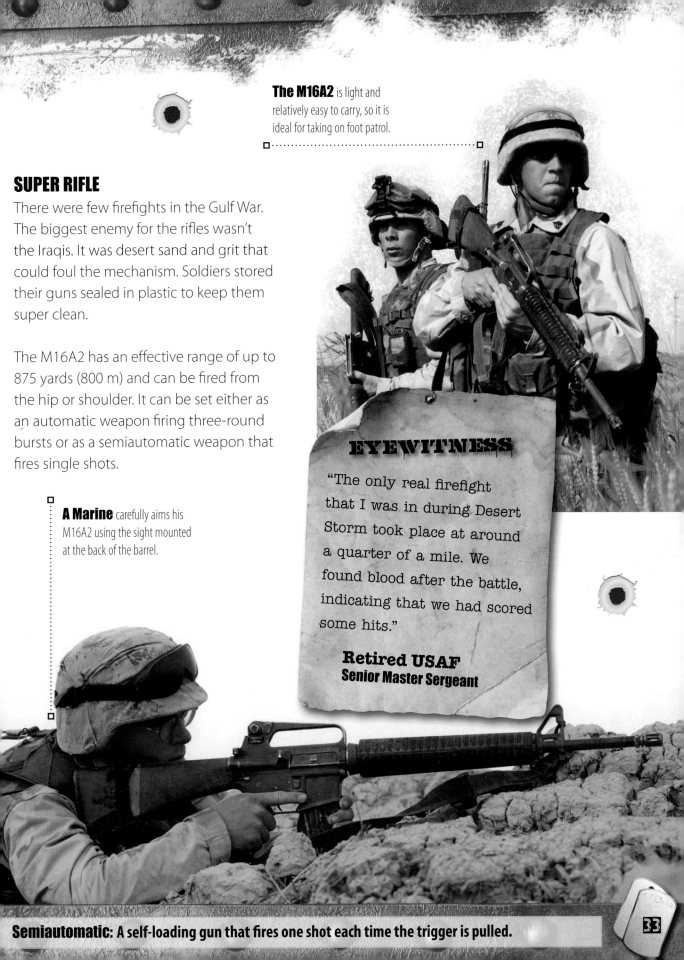

SUPER RIFLE

There were few firefights in the Gulf War. The biggest enemy for the rifles wasn't the Iraqis. It was desert sand and grit that could foul the mechanism. Soldiers stored their guns sealed in plastic to keep them super clean.

The M16A2 has an effective range of up to 875 yards (800 m) and can be fired from the hip or shoulder. It can be set either as an automatic weapon firing three-round bursts or as a semiautomatic weapon that fires single shots.

A Marine carefully aims his M16A2 using the sight mounted at the back of the barrel.

EYEWITNESS

"The only real firefight that I was in during Desert Storm took place at around a quarter of a mile. We found blood after the battle, indicating that we had scored some hits."

**Retired USAF
Senior Master Sergeant**

Semiautomatic: A self-loading gun that fires one shot each time the trigger is pulled.

M109 PALADIN

Few strongholds are safe from the Paladin. The M109 looks a little like a tank, but it's a 155m self-propelled howitzer. Tanks usually fight other tanks. Howitzers more often shell fixed targets. These "bunker busters" have been a backbone of U.S. Army field artillery since the early 1960s. In Operation Desert Storm, howitzers were used for armored artillery raids.

A convoy of Paladins rolls along a road in Iraq in the second Gulf War, in 2003.

Howitzer: A cannon which shoots shells at a low velocity and a high angle of fire.

An M109 (left) is accompanied by a support vehicle for carrying ammunition.

HIT AND RUN

Coalition forces made "hit and run" raids into Iraq and Kuwait. Howitzers attacked targets that needed heavy bombardment to destroy them but were out of reach of guns on battleships in the Persian Gulf. The howitzer got deep into enemy territory and fired its rounds before moving back.

The Paladin was the Gulf War upgrade. Its advanced fire-control system allowed it to fire less than 60 seconds after reaching its target. The U.S. Army had 25 battalions equipped with M109s. In the four-day ground attack, they fired 43,500 rounds.

EYEWITNESS

"I just want everybody to know that we have a toolbox that's full of lots of tools and I brought them all to the party."

General Colin Powell
Chairman, Joint Chiefs of Staff

Watched by his colleagues, a soldier loads a shell into the M109's gun.

Fire-control system: Actions such as loading and aiming that enable a weapon to be fired.

35

MIM-104 PATRIOT

The Patriot missile was the star of the Gulf War. It became a sensation because it could shoot down Iraqi SCUD missiles fired at Saudi Arabia and Israel. Patriot was short for Patriot Tactical Air Defense Missile System. This ground-to-air missile could track, home in on, and destroy incoming missiles in the air.

The Patriot missile is 17.4 feet (5.3 m) long and has a range of 38 miles (60 km).

Tactical: Something related to the immediate action in a conflict, not its overall goals.

A crane unloads containers containing Patriot missiles at an artillery base during Operation Desert Shield.

The missile launchers were mounted on trucks so that they were very maneuverable.

BAPTISM OF FIRE

The Patriot had been tested before, but Operation Desert Storm was its first use in conflict. A lot depended on its success. The Iraqis targeted their neighbors who supported the Coalition. The SCUD missiles could kill a lot of civilians. It was vital they were stopped.

The Patriot's baptism of fire came at the very start of the war. The Iraqis launched their first SCUD attack on January 17, 1991. They fired five missiles. U.S. forces launched two Patriots at every SCUD. They reduced all five to shreds.

SCUD MISSILES

The Patriot's main target was the Iraqis' Soviet-built SCUD missile. These ballistic missiles had a range of about 185 miles (300 km). That brought Iraq's enemies in Israel and Saudi Arabia within range. The Iraqis hid the launchers. They only brought them into the open to fire, then rushed them back under cover from Allied aircraft.

Ballistic: A missile that does not have its own means of propulsion.

EXPLOSIVE

MLRS STEEL RAIN

In a flash of light, a single missile shoots from a launch tube on an MLRS.

Iraqi soldiers dreaded "steel rain." That's what they called the clusters of shells fired by the M270 Multiple Launch Rocket System (MLRS). Whenever the Iraqi command center started to fire, they risked a response from the MLRS. In a few seconds, missiles would rain down on the enemy. The MLRS could fire 12 rockets in only 40 seconds.

Cluster: A group of shells that all fall close to one another at the same time.

STRIKING FEAR

The MLRS was ideal for desert conditions. Carried on a tracked carrier—based on the Bradley Infantry Fighting Vehicle (IFV)—the MLRS could cross the desert at 40 miles per hour (64 km/h).

More than 17,000 rockets were launched in the war. The constant bombardment terrified Iraqi soldiers. The psychological stress was unbearable. Thousands of Iraqis chose to surrender rather than face the "steel rain."

The launcher on this MLRS has been raised into firing position.

Psychological: Something that damages the enemy's spirit rather than causing physical injuries.

TOMAHAWK MISSILE

With a range of 800 miles (1,230 km), the Tomahawk can strike from afar. The Gulf War began with Tomahawk strikes on Iraqi targets fired from U.S. battleships in the Red Sea and Persian Gulf. A Western news correspondent in Baghdad described watching a missile fly down the street outside his hotel.

A trail of smoke marks the path of a Tomahawk fired from the USS *Missouri* at a long-range target.

40

Correspondent: A journalist who reports on a particular subject, such as a war.

A Tomahawk missile blows a warehouse apart in a test exercise.

DEADLY FLIGHT

The war was the first time the Tomahawk had been used in combat. A total of 298 missiles were fired, mainly at strategic targets, such as Iraqi command and control centers.

The missiles do not fly particularly fast. What makes them deadly is that they are hard to detect until it is too late. They fly at very low altitudes and are often used against well-defended targets where an aircraft attack would be risky. Their targets included the headquarters of the Iraqi Air Force in downtown Baghdad.

Command and control center: A position from which commanders direct a conflict.

UAV DRONES

Unmanned aerial vehicles (UAV) may look like model airplanes—but they're deadly serious. These pilotless aircraft were remote-controlled by an operator with a monitor and a controller. The job of the UAV was to take pictures as aerial spies. The images were used to pick out targets for strikes by B-52s or F-15s.

A drone operator uses a handheld monitor to follow the UAV's progress and control its movements.

Remote-controlled: Something that is operated from a distance.

THE SOUND OF FEAR

Iraqi soldiers came to dread the buzzing sound of the Pioneer drone. It meant the bombers were not far behind. There was nowhere to hide. The drone could pick out troops at nighttime or camouflaged vehicles. Once the target had been hit, the drone could take more pictures of the damage inflicted.

At the end of the war, five Iraqi soldiers waved white flags at a drone. It was the first time in history men had surrendered to a robot.

EYEWITNESS

"At least one UAV was airborne at all times during Desert Storm."

Department of Navy Report
May 1991

A soldier launches a small drone at night by throwing it into the air.

WARRIOR INFANTRY FIGHTING VEHICLE

The Warrior IFV was the British Army's answer to the Bradley, but soldiers found it more luxurious than the U.S. vehicle. Its Chobham armor could withstand missiles, RPGs, and even antitank mines. Its job was to keep up with the Challenger tanks over any terrain and to use its firepower to support the infantry during assaults.

A British soldier directs a Warrior into position during Operation Desert Shield.

57 KG 74

RPGs: Rocket-propelled grenades, or small explosives fired from a rocket launcher.

POPULAR VEHICLE

The Warrior's turret turns 360 degrees for observation. The vehicle is armed with a cannon, machine gun, and missile launchers on either side of the turret. It can also be fitted with laser equipment for night fighting. Some troops were more impressed that it comes with its own toilet and with a heater for meals.

During Operation Desert Storm, the Warriors proved very reliable, despite the challenging conditions. None was destroyed by Iraqi missiles, although two were mistakenly destroyed by "friendly fire" from a U.S. A-10 Thunderbolt.

The Warrior's main gun is a 30mm cannon. It can also carry a machine gun, a chain gun, and missile launchers.

FRIENDLY FIRE

The only Warrior IFVs destroyed in the Gulf War were hit by "friendly fire." Two Warriors were destroyed, killing nine UK soldiers. Friendly fire has always existed but in recent decades it has become more frequent. Aircraft increasingly strike from farther away against targets that are sometimes hard to identify for certain.

Turret: A revolving section added to the top of a tank or other military vehicle.

GLOSSARY

armored: Something that is covered with a hard case for protection from missiles.

artillery: Big guns such as cannons, howitzers, and mortars.

automatic: A gun that fires continuously while the trigger is pulled.

cannon: A large-caliber, automatic gun on an airplane.

close air support: Air attacks on enemy weapons or troops fighting on the ground.

coalition: A temporary alliance of countries to achieve a particular purpose.

convoy: An organized group of vehicles or ships all following the same route.

dogfight: A close-quarters fight between warplanes.

fire-control system: Actions such as loading and aiming that enable a weapon to be fired.

guided missile: A missile that can be steered toward its target.

heads-up display: A system that projects data on a level with the pilot's eyes.

howitzer: A cannon that shoots shells at a low velocity and a high angle of fire.

kill range: The distance at which a tank can destroy another tank.

laser: A narrow, high-powered beam of light used to take measurements.

main battle tanks: The most heavily armored and armed class of tanks.

mine: An explosive charge buried in the ground that is detonated by weight.

morale: The spirit of combatants and belief in whether they can win.

multirole: An aircraft that can act as a fighter or a bomber and attack many targets.

radar: A system that locates objects by bouncing radio waves off them.

rifled: A barrel with a spiral groove that spins a shell and makes it more accurate.

SCUD: A Soviet-built ballistic missile that the Iraqis launched against Coalition targets.

semiautomatic: A self-loading gun that fires one shot each time the trigger is pulled.

sortie: A military word for a single mission by a single aircraft.

stealth: Technology designed to minimize an object's visibility to radar.

strategic: Having to do with the overall goals of a military campaign, not the immediate fighting.

tactical: Something related to the immediate action in a conflict, not its overall goals.

FURTHER INFORMATION

BOOKS

Alvarez, Carlos. *M109A6 Paladins* (Torque Books: Military Machines). Bellwether Media, 2009.

Finlan, Alastair. *The Gulf War of 1991*. (Essential Histories: War and Conflict in Modern Times). Rosen Publishing Group, 2008.

Hamilton, John. *Abrams Tanks* (Military Vehicles). Abdo and Daughters, 2011.

Hamilton, John. *UAVs: Unmanned Aerial Vehicles* (Xtreme Military Aircraft). Abdo and Daughters, 2012.

Loveless, Antony. *Apache Helicopter Pilots* (World's Most Dangerous Jobs). Crabtree Publishing Company, 2009.

Parker, Steve. *The M2 Bradley Infantry Fighting Vehicle* (Cross-Sections). Capstone Press, 2007.

Rustad, Martha E. *U.S. Army Infantry Fighting Vehicles* (Blazers: Military Vehicles). Capstone Press, 2006.

Zwier, Lawrence J. and Matthew Scott Weltig. *The Persian Gulf and Iraqi Wars* (Chronicle of America's Wars). Lerner Publishing Group, 2004.

WEBSITES

http://www.desert-storm.com/
General site about the Gulf War, with timelines and pages about weapons.

http://www.pbs.org/wgbh/pages/frontline/gulf/weapons/
PBS site supporting the series *Frontline*, with pages about individual weapons.

http://abcnews.go.com/Technology/story?id=97718&page=1
ABC News page about technology in the Gulf War.

INDEX

A-10 Thunderbolt 6–7
Abrams, M1A1 28–29
AH-1 Supercobra 8–9
AH-64 Apache 10–11
Apache, AH-64 10–11
armor 15, 44
AWACS, E-3 16–17

B-117 Nighthawk 5
B-52 Stratofortress 12–13
Baghdad 22, 25, 41
bombers 12–13, 24–25
Bradley IFV 30–31, 39, 44

Challenger tank 14–15
Coalition 4, 5

drones 42–43

E-3 AWACS 16–17
E-8 Joint STARS 18–19

F-117 Nighthawk 24-25
F-15E Strike Eagle 20–21
F-16 Fighting Falcon 22–23
firefights 33
friendly fire 45

helicopters 8–9, 10–11
Highway of Death 11
howitzers 34–35

Humvee 26–27

infantry 32
Infantry Fighting Vehicles
    30–31, 39, 44–45
intelligence 16, 18–19,
    42–43

Joint STARS, E-8 18–19

Khafji, Battle of 8

M109 Paladin 34–35
M16A2 rifle 32–33
M1A1 Abrams 28, 29
M2/M3 Bradley 30–31
M270 MLRS 38–39
MIM-104 Patriot 36–37
missiles 9, 10, 11, 21, 36–37,
    38–39, 40–41
missiles, SCUD 19, 21, 31, 36,
    37
MLRS 38–39
morale 12, 13

Nighthawk, F-117 24–25

Operation Desert Shield 5
Operation Desert Storm 5,
    13, 17, 20, 25

Paladin 34–35
Pioneer, drone 43

radar 11, 16, 17, 19
rifle, M16A2 32–33

sabots 29
Saddam Hussein 4, 5
Saudi Arabia 4, 5
Schwarzkopf, Norman 18
SCUD missiles 19, 21, 31, 36,
37
stealth technology 24–25
"steel rain" 38, 39
Stratofortress, B-52 12-13
strike aircraft 20–21, 22–23
Strike Eagle, F-15E 20–21
Supercobra, AH-1 8–9

tanks 14–15, 28–29, 31
Thunderbolt, A-10 6–7
Tomahawk missile 40–41

UAV drones 42–43

Vietnam War 9, 32

Warrior IFV 44–45